BaK E

I want to be a
TENNIS PLAYER

By Eugene Baker
Illustrated by Richard Wahl

 CHILDRENS PRESS, CHICAGO

Library of Congress Cataloging in Publication Data

Baker, Eugene H
    I want to be a tennis player.

    SUMMARY: Two children learn to play tennis and
participate in a tournament.
    1. Tennis—Juvenile literature. (1. Tennis)
I. Wahl, Richard, 1939-   illus. II. Title.
GV995.B28   796.34'2   73-738
ISBN 0-516-01746-2

Dave and Diane locked their bikes. "Let's watch," said Dave.

"40-Love." called the big man standing on the tennis court. He threw a ball in the air. ZING! The two players hit the ball back and forth. Finally the big man hit it just beyond the other man's reach.

"That's game and set," smiled the big man. "Thanks for a good game."

The big man looked
around. Many young
people were watching.
"Come in," he called. "It's
time for your first lesson."

When everyone was
seated, he said, "My name
is Jim Hernandez, your teacher.

I see you all have tennis rackets. You also need tennis balls and tennis shoes. The shoes will keep you from slipping."

"This class will learn basic tennis strokes and how to score. The last week we will have a tournament," Jim said.

"That's great!" Dave
said to Diane. He thought
tournaments were fun.

"Now take a ball from
the bag and follow me,"
Jim said.

"This is a diagram of the tennis court. Here is the server's position. The server hits the ball diagonally across the court. The ball *must* land inside the serve court."

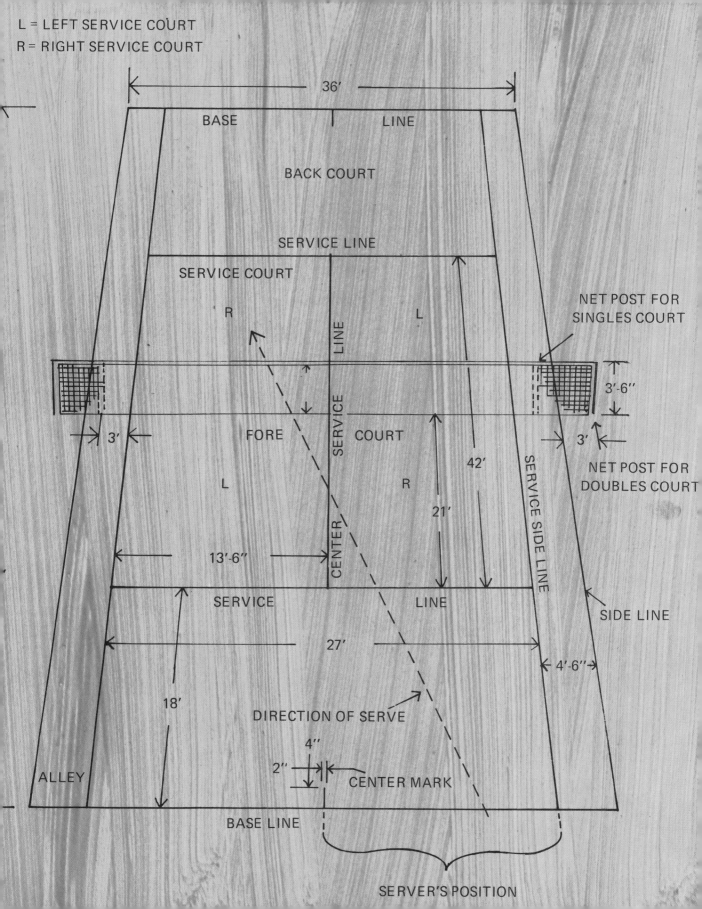

Jim continued. "If the serve is good, the receiver must hit the serve back on the first bounce. The ball is played until someone misses."

"If the first serve is not good, the server gets a second chance. If this one fails, he has made a *double fault.* His opponent gets a point."

"After the first point is scored, the same server moves to the left side of the court. He now serves to the left side of the other court."

"OK. Watch me." Jim said. "Stand with your side toward the net. Toss the ball up. Swing your racket. Hit the ball. To give the ball more speed, let your arm and

racket finish the circle.
This is called a follow
through."

"All right, let's try
it," Jim called.

"Come on Diane, you can
do it," Dave shouted. For
an hour everyone practiced
serving. Jim moved up and
down the court helping.

The next day Jim said, "Today we will learn the forehand stroke. Hit the ball when it nears the top of its bounce. Keep forearm, wrist, and racket in a straight line. Remember, follow through."

For the rest of the week everyone practiced.

"You are doing very well," Jim said. "Now let's try the backhand stroke. Stand with your back a little towards the net. Keep your eyes on the ball. Meet the ball in front of your front foot. Keep your arm straight and follow through."

Diane bounced the ball to Dave. He hit it. POW! The ball sailed over the fence.

"Oh no!" yelled Dave.

"Don't bend your elbow," called Jim.

"Thank you," cried Dave. Then he ran to get his ball.

After weeks of practice, Jim announced, "Tomorrow we start our tournament."

"First, I want to review scoring. A player scores a point when the other player fails to return the ball. To win one game you must score four points. The first point is called 15. The second point is 30. The third point is 40 and the fourth is game point. No points, or 0, is called love. For example, 40-love means the score is 3-0."

15 LOVE	=	**1 - 0**
30 LOVE	=	**2 - 0**
40 LOVE	=	**3 - 0**
GAME POINT	=	**4 - 0**

"If both sides score three points, it is a tie game. To win, one side must score two points in a row. When one player wins six games, a set is finished."

Diane won first place in the girl's match. Dave played well too. But now he was losing 5-4 in games. Everyone was quiet. The ball was in play. Then Dave raced to hit a backhand shot. His ball hit the top net and fell on his side. He lost first place! The final score was 6-4 in games.

Jim Hernandez walked onto the court. "A great match. Will the first and second place winners come up and get your trophies."

"Come on, Diane," said Dave. "Let's get our trophies for mom. She'll really be proud of us."

About the Author:
Dr. Baker was graduated from Carthage College, Carthage, Illinois. He got his master's degree and doctorate in education at Northwestern University. He has worked as a teacher, as a principal, and as a director of curriculum and instruction. Now he works full time as a curriculum consultant. His practical help to schools where new programs are evolving is sparked with his boundless enthusiasm. He likes to see social studies and language arts taught with countless resources and many books to encourage students to think independently, creatively, and critically. The Bakers, who live in Arlington Heights, Illinois, have a son and two daughters.

About the Artist:
Richard Wahl, graduate of the Art Center College of Design in Los Angeles, has illustrated a number of magazine articles and booklets. He is a skilled artist and photographer who advocates realistic interpretations of his subjects. He lives with his wife and small son in Evanston, Illinois.